SON OF BRISTLE

A second guide to what the natives say and mean
in the heart of the Wess Vinglun

Edited by
DIRK ROBSON
using an old garden-rake

and illustrated by
VIC WILTSHIRE
wielding a sharp knife and fork

Abson Books   Abson   Wick   Bristol

For my mother
(*who always keeps her guid Scots accent*)

ABSON BOOKS Abson Wick Bristol
First published in Great Britain, October 1971

© Derek Robinson

All rights reserved
No part of this book, either text or illustrations,
may be reproduced in any form without the
written consent of the publishers.

Printed by Burleigh Ltd., at the Burleigh Press, Bristol 1

SBN 902920 03 0

FOREWORD

I am delighted to recommend this useful little book, because the author has promised to pay me if I do—not much money, to be sure, but then it's not much of a book and besides, I'm not much of a recommendation.

In fact, when you get right down to it, I suppose neither the book nor myself is really worth a fraction of the amounts involved. What's more, if any of us had a scrap of decency or an ounce of honesty in our decadent, crumbling bodies we would never allow ourselves to get involved in such a lousy, crumby little deal as this.

My God! They must think I've fallen pretty low if they expect me to risk my reputation over their cheap bit of catchpenny trash, all for a mere pittance! Listen here, Robson, you bum—I wouldn't tout your tatty pamphlets for you if you gave me a thousand quid, d'you hear that?

What d'you think I am, some sort of cheap hypocrite? Get lost, and take your garbage with you. I have never read your grubby little book, but I know one thing for sure. It stinks. (And you can quote me on that.)

J. GRIMSBY FISH
Divorce Enquiries
Lawnmowers Ground and Set
Private Tap-Dance Lessons

This is a work of fiction (although—in a greater sense—are we not *all* works of fiction?). Any similarity between any character and any person living or dead is purely coincidental; and if you think you can detect any such resemblance, my advice to you is to nip round and see the doctor first thing in the morning.

THE AUTHOR

For many years it was thought that Dirk Robson concealed the true identity of Dr Stanley Grunge, a former professional octopus-wrestler who was given the Chair of Advanced Reaction at Bristle University after he had loudly admired it at a party. However, the untimely loss of Dr Grunge (found sprawled on his library floor with a ghastly expression on his face and a pickled onion stuffed up each nostril) made it necessary to reconsider this view; and it is now thought likely that Dirk Robson is really Lady Flossy Strop-Fetlock, the only woman on record who has kicked a Rugby ball across the Thames while holding a glass of sherry in each hand. She is also the only woman known to have addressed the Dutch Parliament in fluent Burmese, and vice versa. Lady Flossy has been married seven times, five of them to the bandleader Dudley Trubshaw and twice to a completely different Dudley Trubshaw whom she mistook for the bandleader because it was so dark at the time. She has a size-6 foot and wears size-4 shoes which hurt incessantly. She rarely appears in public, because people often mistake her for the *other* Flossy Strop-Fetlock (the one who feeds her begonias on scrambled egg, and then sings); and this she finds awfully sad, somehow.

PREFACE

This book is a sequel to 'Krek Waiter's Peak Bristle'. Behind them both lies a curious story.

When 'Krek Waiter's Peak Bristle' first came out, several bookshops stocked it under the impression that it was a Greek phrase-book for tourists, and many customers bought it under the impression that it was a load of old rubbish (but cheap at the price).

Startled by this success, the publishers blew the profits on a long weekend at Severn Beach. They got back to find on the doormat a demand note from the Inland Revenue. Searching the premises for something to pawn, they came across three tons of plain paper in the billiard room. It was lightly mildewed at the edges but still quite firm in the centre.

An hour later I received a telegram: PLEASE WRITE SMALL CHEAP BESTSELLER STOP NO PORN STOP DON'T JUST SIT THERE WITH YOUR MOUTH OPEN GET CRACKING STOP.

The result was 'Son of Bristle'. Many people did their best to discourage me. "For God's sake, no," wrote the Bishop of Peebles. "Haven't you done enough damage already?" demanded Dame Flora Couchgrass, the vegetarian and former roller-skate sprint champion. "Just watch it," warned Dudley Grunge (24) of Slough.

Outright intimidation followed. Hostile women jostled me at

jumble sales, and I was savagely hacked on the shins while playing Rugby. The roof of my car was repeatedly fouled by trained pigeons, some probably Communists.

Nevertheless, 'Son of Bristle' was completed, and here it is—a load of brand-new rubbish, but still cheap at the price.

Dirk Robson
Red Lun, Bristle, July 1971

EUREKAL! The famous Bristle L

Bristle is the only city in Britain to be able to turn ideas into ideals, areas into aerials, and Monicas into monocles.

Nobody knows why the Bristle folk slap an L on the end of any and every word which offers a conveniently overhanging 'a' or 'o' sound, but they do, and it's been going on for a long time. 'Bristle' itself was made out of *brig* (bridge) and *stowe* (place) plus a final L to keep the dust out.

Probably the most famous result of the Bristle L was the city father who had three lovely daughters, Idle, Evil and Normal. (To these can be added three other uniquely Bristle girls: Annal, Martial and Monocle.) But without a doubt the most telling demonstration of the Bristle L took place a couple of years ago when a television crew recorded several citizens while they read aloud the words on a theatre poster, which turned out to be featuring Eval Turner, Primal Donnal of the Carl Rosal Operal. It goes without saying that the company performed such works as Aidal, La Traviatal, Rigolettol, and Cavalerial Rusticanal.

Few foreign countries are safe from the Bristle L. It ranges the world, from Nigerial to Malaysial, from Bolivial to Australial, from Costal Rical to the Costal Braval. It affects Canadal and American (for which you need a visal) as well as the notorious malarial areal of Africal.

But it is in everyday life that the Bristle L flourishes. A local girl who was learning to dance was heard to say, "I can rumble but I can't tangle." Bristle housewives go shopping for bananals, semolinal, tinned tunal fish, and a Victorial sandwich, as well as Ryvital and Ambrosial creamed rice. Kitchen tops are covered with Formical. Sinks are cleaned with ammonial.

Hardly anything in the garden escapes—begonials, fuschials, dahlials, hydrangeals, even aspidistrals. And not even diseases are immune. People in Bristle have been struck down by the grisly influenzal and pneumonial. Happily, diphtherial is rare, although visitors should beware the dreaded Dire Eel.

Neither television nor religion offers any escape from the Bristle L. You're just as likely to find yourself watching Panoramal, or a programme from Granadal, or a re-run of the Forsyte Sagal; and if you go to church it will probably turn out to be either St Teresal's, St Helenal's, St Brendal's or St Kildal's.

You can always get in your car and drive away, of course. Just make sure it isn't a Cortinal, Anglial, Simcal, Lancial, Hondal, Toyotal, Alfal-Romeol, Vival, Volvol, eteceteral, etceteral, etceteral.

SON OF BRISTLE

Annuity: Claim to insight; as in: 'Annuity was line, cuzzy turn dread.'

Ant Eye: Appeal for support, usually tacked on to end of sentence; as in: 'Core sigh can't goat the pitchers. Gotta state tome an mine the baby, ant eye?'

Am Rim: Cry uttered by spectators at Rugby match whenever opponent gets the ball.

Ashen Core: Former stately home, still standing in rolling parkland near Long Ashen.

Beers Port: Ancient chant, traditionally uttered by the natives in order to bring about a change of fortune. Rarely successful.

Beet Root Chew: Declaration of faithfulness; as in: 'I'll always beet root chew, luv.'

Bit Rend: Unpleasant outcome.

Bren Jam: Popular food item.
Bristle Grams Cool: Local academy for boys.
Buffer: Had circumstances been otherwise; as in: 'Buffer rim, she'd bean side a nurse gnome now.'
Bum Tinto: Met by chance; as in: 'Guess why bum tinto in Shrampton smorning?'
Butt Knoll: Small slit in clothing.

Canteen: Measure of extreme inability; as in: 'Fat? He canteen seize zone feet knee more!'
Carnival: Warning against greed; as in: 'Yer, you carnival them straw breeze!'
Cease: Chairs.
Cess Rees: Extra items, e.g. gloves, handbags, earrings, etc. Sometimes known as 'Matchin Cess Rees', which cost 25% more.
Chess: Upper part of body, e.g. Chess Eggs Ray.
Clift Nice Cool: Bristle's answer to Roedean.
Clyde: Run into.
Corsairs; Corsets: These words usually introduce a confident claim, such as: 'Corsairs moron one waiters kin a cat.' Or: 'Corsets knotter real usban, juno.'

Deck Rating: Painting and wallpapering.
Dennis: Tooth doctor.
Dummy: Phrase meaning 'completed my'; as in: 'Tell meal laughter wait—I can't seam till eye dummy pools.'
Dwight Elm Outer: Start of retaliatory remark tinged with indignation; as in: 'Wine tea mined zone business? Aft trawl, dwight elm outer do *is* job?'

Earner: Expression of feminine contempt; as in: 'Ooze she kidding wither big eye deals? Earner count's louse!'
Ev Smuch: A great deal, a lot. **Ev S'** is the universal term of emphasis in Bristle. For example, 'Ev Sgood' means anything from 'not bad' to 'fantastic'. Other Ev-words are: Ev Snice, Ev Seasy, Ev Soften, Ev Sot, Ev Scold, Ev Sweat, Ev Slate, Ev Sold and Ev Sevvy.

Fairy Nuff: Expression of satisfaction, based on the wellknown passion of the Little Folk for British justice. (For the benefit of those unfamiliar with the world of elves and pixies, Fairy Nuff was the one in Enid Blyton with red hair and freckles, who was victimised when Noddy circulated false rumours of drunkenness and shoplifting and had her hounded out of the Union. It was in all the papers.)
Feud: Beginning of suggestion; as in: 'Feud shrup a mint, you'd seat eye mean.' A similar opening is **Fuel**; as in: 'Fuel grout an shove, I'll stain side and steer.'
Fig Red: Statue at sharp end of ship.
Finch: End; as in: 'Ant chew finched yet?'
Fine: Discover.
Fought: Considered.
Four Stout: Ejected by force; as in this typical piece of Rugby commentary: '... annie nearly scores butties four stout ...'
Freeze A Bird: Completely at liberty.

Ginger: Start of question concerning wellbeing; as in:
   A. 'Scold out smornin—Ice lipped onna payment.'
   B. 'Ginger yourself?'
Gnat Case: In those circumstances.

Gnome: Claim acquaintance with; as in: 'Gnome? Coarse eye gnome! We bin mace for munce!'

Grape Ride: Much self-esteem.

Grape Written: England, Ireland, Scotland and Wales. The **S.S. Grape Written** is in dry dock in Bristle.

Greyful: Appreciative. **Moron Greyful:** Highly appreciative.

Groan Pains: Childhood discomfort.

Gross Rees: Household goods sold in, e.g. supermarket.

Guard Nose: Horticultural equipment.

Guess Tuck Interim: Advice uttered by spectators at football match, esp. when player appears reluctant to engage whole-heartedly in the action.

Guise: (see **Scouse**.)

Ice Pecked: Suggest a likelihood; as in: 'Ice pecked ease gone infra beer.'

Ice Pose; Ice Poseys; Ice Poser: Suggest a possibility, as in:
'Snot on telly, ice pose?'
'Ice poseys gone wafer is oll daze.'
'Ice poser dad wooden letter seam again.'

Instant: Happening, event.

Into: Not very; as in: 'She into good at sums, butter jogger fee slot better.'

Isolate: Indicates reluctance to act; as in: 'Isolate moon away from Bristle. Aft trawl, swear I grup, innit?'

Jubilee: Question of opinion; as in: 'Jubilee view should stake wyatt? Or jubilee vince pekin your mine?'

Juicy: Word used to introduce an inquiry about something taking place; as in:

'Juicy what icy?'
or 'Juicy the nude reins bean laid inna necks treat?'

Lady Slavs: Half of a public convenience.
Lass Mint: Very late; urgent.
Lay Bricks Change: Department of Employment.
Lean Tomb: Recommendation of non-interference; as in: 'Yer! You lean tomb self, rile beacher red in!' A similar phrase is **Lean Lone**; as in: 'That paint sweat—lean lone!'
Lecher: Permissive advice; as in: 'Wine chew guess tuck inter the scrumpy, an lecher rare down?'
Lessee: Note of caution; as in:
  A. Started train—we might swell goat the pitchers.
  B. Well, lessee fits gonny buddy good knit, first.
Libel: Likely or inclined; as in: 'Coal Snaw's libel to be soul doubt.'
Lice: Illuminations. These take many forms, such as Head Lice (on cars) and Street Lice (in public places).
Lice Witch: Device for controlling lice. However, a **Lice Plit** is an alcoholic beverage.
Line: Dishonest; as in: 'Ease line, yeronner!'
Log Reds: Deadlock.
Lonely Bee: Understatement; as in:
  'Yukon stain a car few like—lonely bee tie mince.'
  or: 'Jew wanna comfortee? It lonely bee bren jam, ice pecked.'
Loss: Large quantities; plenty.

McNubbout: Many words owe their origins to surnames. 'Hooligan' came from a delinquent Irish family in London, the

O'Hulihans. The Earl of Sandwich invented the packed lunch, Wellington gave us the boot, and it was a Brighton greengrocer (and amateur inventor) by the name of W. C. Flush who perfected the modern toilet; while we owe the word 'harass' to a notoriously persistent rent-collector in 18th-century Lancashire, one Zebedee Harris.

Bristle's contribution to this list comes from a Scottish kilt-manufacturer, Hamish McNubbout (1753–1829) who came south and established a business in Reckliff. Demand for kilts in that part of Bristle was slight, and Hamish McNubbout found himself with so much time on his hands that eventually his name became a byword for idling. When asked by their parents what they had been up to, kids used to mumble: 'Juss McNubbout.' In those days they usually got a clip on the ear for not speaking properly.

Major: Reflection on some other person's behaviour, as in: 'Ant chew major mine dup yet?'

Mill: Centre.

Mine: Intellect.

Mine Jew: Take into account.

Neck Store: Neighbouring.

Neuter: Unfamiliar with; as in:
 A. 'How dye getta Gloss Trode?'
 B. 'Dunno, I'm neuter Bristle.'

Nice Cool: Evening institute.

Nose Snot: Negative reply; as in:
 A. Din ronna table yet?
 B. Nose snot.

Office Ed: Daft. The original Office Ed was a clerk named Edward Upjohn, who worked in a Chinese spaghetti factory in Bemmister. People used to get drunk and telephone him in the middle of the night, saying: 'Are you up, John?' It drove him daft.
Oliver Sun: Unexpectedly.
Ooze Pain: Query about source of money.

Pasture: This way; as in: 'Scene knee numb rate buses go pasture?'
Plea Scar: Panda.
Plover: Kind of sweater.
Prayed: March-past.

Ray-Joe Bristle: Local broadcasting station with two DJ's, Ray Gin-Eddake and Joe Kinnapart.
Relay: Emphatic response indicating mild astonishment; as in:
    A. 'Ant chew erred? Easy loped wither from neck store!'
    B. 'No! Relay?'
Rival: Entry.
Rub Sheep: Pile of garbage.

Scampi: Statement of impossibility; as in: 'This scampi wary lives—scot no lice on.'
Scene Sow: Under the prevailing conditions; as in: 'Scene sow ease always onna beer, snow under he puss on smuch weight.'
Scouse: (see **Guise**.)
Seizure: It's not so difficult; as in: 'One shoe guess tarted, seizure knit looks.'

Senior: Start of personal enquiry; as in: 'Senior dad knee wear? Ease poster mimi yer quart van our ago.'
Serfs: The outside area.
Shane Cream; Shane Soap: Male toiletries.
Short Urn: You're next.
Sickle Downer: Nauseated; as in: 'R Normal went honour Sunny's Cool out-in yesdee, and she was sickle downer teacher's plover.'
Sikh Debts: Teenage sailors.
Skills: Pub game.
Smite Urn: I'm next.
Snow Under: I'm not surprised.
Sordid Doubt: Cleared up, explained; as in: 'Saul micks tup—summoned better sordid doubt.'
Sparky: Snot ott.
Stans Treason: Commonsense indicates.
Story Cheaters: Way of keeping the house warm.
Stray Ford: Simple, honest, uncomplicated.
Strew: That's right.
Sum Set: Neighbouring county.
Sup Chew Knit: Passing the buck. For example:
    A. 'Waddle eye sate rim, fee guess fresher summit?'
    B. 'Sup chew, knit?'

Tale Tense: Ping-pong.
Tall Deep Ends: Praps. On the other hand, praps not.
Tour Free: Less than 4.
Toes Track: Device for keeping burnt bread cold at breakfast.

Waddle Eye Sate: see **Sup Chew Knit**.

Wafer: see **Ice Poseys**.
Wane: Entrance.
Wine Tea: see **Dwight Elm Outer**.
Wodge: Opening word of cross-examination; as in: 'Wodge you mean bite?'
Word: Anxious.
Work Knee; Work Nigh: Enquiries concerning whereabouts; for example:
　'Work knee parky scar?'
　'Work nigh see the prayed?'
Worm Stew: Further enquiry concerning whereabouts; for example:
　A. 'Pretty ice lated yer, incher? Worms stew gopher yer gross rees?'
　B. 'Bout mile naff, ice pose. Mine jew, the misses bake slot.'
Wreck Ross: International disaster-relief agency.

Yule Laughter: Opening words of command or requirement; as in: 'Yule laughter buyer summit—aft trawl, sir birthday.' See also **Dummy**.
Yuma: Lead-in to descriptive remark, such as:
　'Yuma secker tree yer, incher?'
　or: 'Yuma lines wine!'

ACKNOWLEDGEMENTS

Nobody helped me compile this book; I did it all myself, except for the pictures, which Vic Wiltshire drew (brilliantly).

In particular, I got no help from SWEB, who supply such feeble power to this part of Bristle that even my chilblains got frostbite last winter; from the Inland Revenue, who persist on taxing me on the money I haven't yet made as well as on the money I've already spent; from the licensing laws, which make me drink when I'm not thirsty and leave me thirsty when I need a drink; from the pigeons in the attic overhead, who play football and perform clog-dances while I'm trying to work; from the kids next door, who keep waking me up while I'm pretending to think; from Bill Fry, who declines to let me beat him at squash; and above all from J. Grimsby Fish, who ratted on me after I had given him five bob as agreed.

Have you read Dirk Robson's first hilarious, best-selling Bristle book—**Krek Waiter's Peak Bristle** (Correct Way To Speak Bristol)? Krek Waiter's Peak Bristle and Son of Bristle are the essential kit for living and laughing in and out of Bristol.

Each book costs 33p and is obtainable from all bookshops and newsagents, or post free from the publishers, Abson Books Abson, Wick, Bristol BS15 5TT.

Other Abson Books include:—

American English/English American 30p—a two-way turn-over glossary of everyday words which have completely different meanings depending on which side of the Atlantic you happen to be.

Sleepless Sleepers 20p—60 ways of overcoming insomnia.

Rhyming Cockney Slang, with illustrations 25p.

Cooking Courgettes/Zucchini/Baby Marrows with gift packet of seeas 27p.

 Abson Wick Bristol England